# PASSIVE SOLAR

# SIMPLIFIED

Easily design a truly green home
for Colorado and the West

by Thomas Doerr

Alítheia Press

Passive Solar Simplified; Easily design a truly green home for Colorado and the West

ISBN: 1452856575
EAN-13: 978-1452856575

Library of Congress Control Number: 2010907190

Alitheia Press
AlitheiaPress.com

Printed in the United States of America

First Edition, July 2012
10 9 8 7 6 5 4 3 2 1

"Why wouldn't you want a passive solar house? This book thoroughly explores one of the simplest and most powerful ideas in the world."

-Bill McKibben, founder of 350.org

"While I'm deep in the photovoltaic and renewable energy world, a holistic approach demands that you start with energy efficiency and passive technologies, then 'fill in the gaps' with renewable energy. *Passive Solar Simplified* is a good book for anyone designing a home."

-Sam Ley, PV Design Engineer

# CONTENTS

# LIST OF TABLES

## ACKNOWLEDGEMENTS

I warmly thank everyone who helped me research and write this book, especially Caroline Kert, Peter Criscione, Andrew Berg, Claire Lay, Scott Perlman, and Eric Doub. For walking the green talk, I want to thank all my wonderful clients, especially Ann and Mike Moore, Holle Finch, Erik Bien, Beverly Jackson, Cindy Troxell, Dan Murphy, and Vahe Derounian.

This book is dedicated to my beautiful daughters, Sophia and Charissa, and to all our children's futures.

# ABOUT THE AUTHOR

Internationally experienced, award-winning architect Thomas Doerr specializes in sustainable design, including passive solar, net-zero energy, and off-grid homes. Thomas has designed successful projects as large as hotels and as small as light fixtures. His designs have been published in magazines, received professional awards, and exhibited in galleries.

Thomas Doerr

Thomas is a Green Points certified architect and past chair of the Colorado chapter of the AIA's (American Institute of Architects) Committee on the Environment. He authored the Green Architecture Checklist for residences, edited the commercial checklist, and he helped edit the Rocky Mountain edition of The Sustainable Design Resource Guide. Thomas is a licensed Energy Efficiency Inspector contractor and is a professional advisor for the US Green Building Council's (USGBC) Green Home Guide.

After working at firms in Austin, Boston, San Francisco, Germany, and Denver; Thomas founded his own firm, Doerr Architecture, to offer high-quality, ecological, and personal service.

Thomas earned a professional degree in architecture from the University of Texas at Austin; studied architecture in Rome, Italy with Temple University; and then earned a master of architecture degree from the University of California at Berkeley. He has taught architecture at the University of Colorado and green building at Naropa University. He is a frequent speaker at green building conferences.

Thomas lives in Boulder, Colorado with his wonderful family. His friends speculate on which will kill him first, his mountain biking or his absurd dancing.

Learn more and find contact information to send your questions or comments to at BuildSustainably.com.

# OVERVIEW OF PASSIVE SOLAR

We want to save money, ensure our family's comfort, and be less of an impact on the planet. Our homes can help us do all this if they are designed to be passive solar. Most know that passive solar design can be used to heat homes, but it can do more. Passive solar can also be used to cool, light, and ventilate homes. It can do all this without burning fossil fuels or causing nuclear waste. Passive solar is the foundation of a truly green home.

The sun has abundant, clean, free energy. This book will show you how to take advantage of passive solar energy in your home to:

- Save energy costs
- Lessen your dependence on volatile energy sources
- Improve your health
- Tread more lightly on the earth

Passive solar design will save a great deal of energy, which will save a great deal of money. Passive solar can save over 80 percent of the heating and cooling costs of your home—a great investment, especially in today's volatile markets. Americans spend about $2000 per year for energy for their homes and this is sure to soon increase dramatically as old energy sources dwindle, demand for them increases, and prices skyrocket.

Much of passive solar design costs nothing and using it will help you avoid common mistakes. You can save more money on energy costs than you would spend on the additional cost to a home loan for the passive solar elements, a no brainer. This why many lenders will qualify you for a larger loan on an energy efficient house. Passive solar design even saves money on expensive systems. For example, passive solar can reduce the size and cost of the backup furnace and the active solar systems.

With passive solar, you can ensure your home's comfort by making it less dependent on traditional energy sources, which can be disrupted. Passive solar design will ensure your home is comfortably heated, cooled, lighted, and ventilated, even if the power lines go down. If your power goes out in the winter, your home will be warm so that your family and the pipes do not freeze. You can go to Jamaica all winter and come back to a home that has stayed warm without burning any fossil fuels to do so. Passive solar design also ensures that your home is much more comfortable in the summer.

With a passive solar home's health-giving daylighting, connection to the seasons, thermal comfort, and superior indoor air quality, it can improve your health. Passive solar design works with nature, instead of against it.

Passive solar will help you tread lightly on the earth because you will not need to burn much fossil fuel or create nuclear waste to meet your home's energy needs. Every home is solar heated, for better or for worse. This book is about how to do it better.

> "Don't get me wrong: I love nuclear energy! It's just that I prefer fusion to fission. And it just so happens that there's an enormous fusion reactor safely banked a few million miles from us. It delivers more than we could ever use in just about eight minutes. And it's wireless!"
>
> -William McDonough

Passive solar will help you live more sustainably. Sustainability ensures that our decisions and actions today do not destroy the opportunities of future generations. In other words, sustainability means ensuring that our great-great-grandchildren have the same energy options and beautiful planet that we have.

Of all the energy that Americans use, almost half of it goes into buildings according to Architecture 2030 (Figure 1.1). Building energy use is greater than both transportation and industrial uses, so do not be too pleased with yourself for driving a hybrid car if your home is an energy hog.

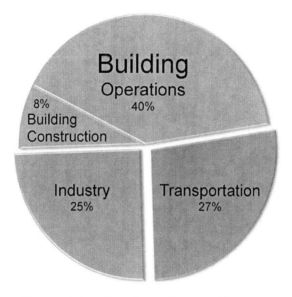

Figure 1.1 American Energy Use — building operations and construction account for about half of it.

Over 98 percent of scientists agree that this energy use is causing global climate change by releasing to the upper atmosphere greenhouse gasses, mostly carbon dioxide, or $CO_2$. According to the US Department of Energy, in 2006 the world created 29.2 billion metric tons of carbon dioxide. The US, with only five percent of world population, created 5.9 billion metric tons, or 20 percent, of this. Our energy use also causes depletion of non-renewable fuels and increased damage from their extraction and use; habitat destruction; loss of biodiversity; and pollution of our air, water, and land. It need not be this way.

Even with the enormous quantity of energy that humans use today, the sun currently provides the Earth 10,000 times more energy than this. We just need to use it. Passive solar design uses the sun's energy and will save money, your health, and *hopefully* the planet.

Plus, passive solar design is simply not that complicated. You do not need a degree in physics to understand and apply this knowledge successfully. This little book is not a complicated treatise on exotic theories of passive solar with byzantine formulas. Instead, it is a straightforward and concise, yet complete, guide to the tried and true passive solar methods that will save you energy. This book has just what you need to know.

One of the reasons why even most architects do not use passive solar design is because the books about it are usually confusing or oversimplified, if not wrong. This book was written to correct this unfortunate situation with complete and reliable information, presented clearly and concisely.

## DEFINITIONS

Let's clarify a few things.

**Passive solar** is the non-mechanical use of sunlight in a building for heating, cooling, lighting, and ventilation—Low-tech.

**Active solar** is the use of mechanical equipment and sunlight to create electricity or hot water—High-tech.

> **PV** is photovoltaic—active solar used to create electricity, also called solar electric.

> **Solar thermal** is active solar used to create hot water, also called solar hot water.

Both passive and active solar are used in the Finstad+Cash House (Figures 1.2, 3.13). Doerr Architecture designed this house to use both passive and active solar in order to be off-grid (not connected to any outside utilities), even at an elevation of 9000 feet in the Rocky Mountains of Colorado. It is an improved version of the old earthship. It will supply all of its own heating, cooling, electricity, water, and waste disposal. Its passive solar system (direct gain) includes the properly shaded and sized southern windows. You can see its active solar in its solar thermal panels, which create hot water. The PV panels, which create electricity, are on a detached garage.

Figure 1.2 The Finstad+Cash House, which uses both passive and active solar, was designed to be off-grid. You can see the passive solar system's properly shaded and sized southern windows and you can see its active solar panels on the lower left roof. Image by Courtland Gross.

Passive solar effectively has just one moving part, the sun. (Yes, it's really our planet's movement that is significant, but you know what I mean.) Active solar is great, but only when used to accomplish what you did not accomplish with simple, inexpensive passive solar. Think of active solar as icing on the cake; first, you want a good cake of passive solar, including energy efficient construction.

Figure 1.3 Passive solar homes can even look quite conventional, like the Troxell+Murphy House in Boulder, Colorado, designed by Doerr Architecture. The clients wanted to fit in to their neighborhood of spec homes.

The passive solar techniques in this book are for residences and they could also be used in other buildings such as small office and retail buildings, schools, libraries, medical offices, and warehouses. Most other commercial and institutional buildings would need to modify these techniques significantly since these building types generate much internal heat per external building surface.

This book is written for Colorado and the western states between latitudes 34° and 45° north, with their ideal climate for passive solar. Since the following states have similar winter temperatures, relative humidity, solar radiation (insolation), and latitude, these passive solar techniques would work well for Utah, Nevada, and Wyoming, as well as parts of New Mexico, Arizona, California, Oregon, Nebraska, Texas, Oklahoma, Kansas, Idaho, and South Dakota. Houses for other regions would need to alter their passive solar techniques. An architect who specializes in passive solar design can determine the right techniques for your climate and building type.

Solar homes don't have to look like the goofy stuff built in the 1970s. They can be built in any style, from Tudor to Southwestern to contemporary, and they can be quite beautiful. None of the passive solar systems or strategies you will learn about will be any good if the house is ugly because, if it is ugly, no one is going to want to live there and it will be torn down. So, as you design your passive solar home, use proportion, scale, rhythm, color, and all the other aesthetic tools to make it beautiful.

# CHAPTER II

# THE THREE PASSIVE SOLAR SYSTEMS

All passive solar systems rely on energy from the sun. Passive solar works like a garden's greenhouse or a car on a hot day with its windows rolled up.

Figure 2.1 Passive solar energy. The sun sends short wavelength energy (light) through the collector (usually glass), it then hits a solid absorber, which converts it into long wavelength energy (heat), that can then be trapped in the space.

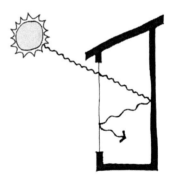

There are three main types of passive solar systems: direct gain, thermal storage walls, and sunspaces. We will go over these three passive solar systems in detail starting with the least complex. Keep in mind that you can, and often should, use more than one of these passive solar systems in one building; they are not mutually exclusive.

## DIRECT GAIN SYSTEMS

The first type of passive solar system this book will cover is direct gain. Direct gain systems are the least complex and the most common. Direct gain is also the least expensive passive solar system, since it uses the windows, walls, and floors of the home for the system instead of requiring separate elements.

To heat a home in the winter with direct gain systems, the southern sun's heat is allowed in through the solar collector (southern glass) and it is absorbed mainly by the home's floors and walls (Figure 2.2). The area of southern glass is determined with Table 3.2.

Cooling is achieved by opening high and low windows to allow convection (hot air rising, or the stack effect) to take hot air up and out, creating a vacuum that pulls cool air through the house.

To cool and heat a house well with a direct gain passive solar system, the high summer sun's rays (energy) must be blocked, the low winter sun's rays must be allowed in, and the winter heat must be stored for the night. This can be easily achieved with solar shading and thermal mass, which will be described in chapter three.

## DIRECT GAIN

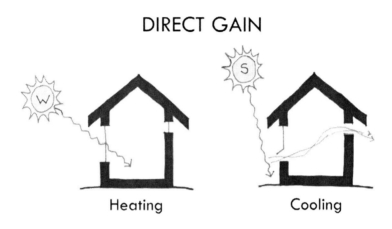

Heating                Cooling

Figure 2.2    Direct Gain System. In the winter (Heating) solar radiation goes through the collectors (windows) and directly heats the living space's absorbers (floors and walls). During the summer (Cooling), solar radiation is blocked and hot air rises out of the building, which pulls cool air through.

An example of a direct gain system is the Moore NZE House in the Rocky Mountains of Colorado (Figure 2.3). NZE (Net-zero energy, zero net energy, or ZNE) homes create more energy than they use. The Moore NZE house is at an elevation of almost 8,000 feet and was designed by Doerr Architecture. This house captures the winter sunlight with its southern windows and stores this energy in its thick plaster on double gypsum board walls and its tile floors (Figure 2.4). It has high windows to let out summer heat and pull cool night air through the interior (Figure 3.14). Blocking summer sunlight was done with the traditional Southwestern architectural elements of vigas (rough wood beams) with cross members (Figure 3.4).

Figure 2.3 The Moore NZE House's direct gain system uses its southern windows as solar collectors.

The US Department of Energy's Energy Star program states that a typical new house will score 100 on its HERS (Home Energy Rating System). The lower a house scores, the less energy it uses. Along with super-insulation and active solar, the direct gain passive solar system in the Moore NZE House earned it an amazing HERS score of -3, one of the only houses to ever score this well.

After the Moore NZE House creates enough extra energy to 'pay off' the carbon debt of its construction, it will be a carbon neutral building. If all buildings were carbon neutral, global climate change would be stopped.

Figure 2.4 The Moore NZE House's direct gain system uses its walls and floors as solar absorbers and thermal storage.

## THERMAL STORAGE WALL SYSTEMS

The second type of passive solar system this book will cover is the thermal storage wall (also called trombe walls and mass walls). Thermal storage walls rely on conduction (like touching a warm tea cup) to transfer heat through a dense material into the living space (Figure 2.5). Thermal storage wall systems are the most common indirect gain system.

# THERMAL STORAGE WALL

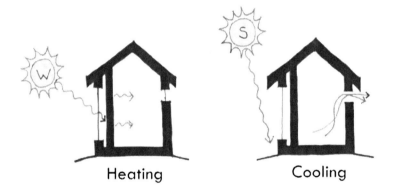

Heating          Cooling

Figure 2.5 Thermal Storage Wall System. In the winter (Heating) the sun's energy goes through the collector (glass), hits an absorber (mass wall), and the heat is then conducted through the absorber into the living spaces. In summer (Cooling), the sun's energy is blocked from the collector and hot air rises out of the building, which pulls cool air through.

Thermal storage walls are great when you want more privacy or less daylight in a living space because they have fewer windows to the living spaces. They also allow more wall area than direct gain systems.

Thermal storage walls use a south facing solar collector, usually double-paned glass, 2-6 inches in front of a mass wall that has a dark surface facing the glass. The area of southern glass is determined with Table 3.2. This mass wall should be 10-18 inches thick; the greater the thickness, the less temperature fluctuation. For most wall materials, 12-14 inches of thickness works well. One inch of mass wall delays the heat from entering the living space by about one hour. Mass walls are often made of grout-filled concrete blocks, but can be stone, concrete, brick, and other dense materials (see chapter three).

Thermal storage walls systems require the building to be narrower than 24 feet deep so that heat from the south side of the house gets to the north side.

An example of a thermal storage wall system is NREL's (National Renewable Energy Laboratory) Visitors Center (Figure 2.6) in Golden, Colorado designed by Anderson DeBartolo Pan. Behind the Visitor Center's southern glass are filled concrete block mass walls to absorb the sun's energy and delay its heat from reaching the occupied space. The

Visitor Center's tall glass collectors are protected from the summer sun with the grid of white solar shades.

Figure 2.6 Example of thermal storage wall. NREL's Visitors Center in Golden, Colorado. NREL also has direct gain in the same space. Photo courtesy of NREL.

To get daylight and more immediate heat in the morning, the Visitors Center also has direct gain in the same space. Since the direct gain collectors heat the space for the day, the thermal storage walls absorb the sun's energy to keep the space warm in the evening. Because the Visitors Center is not occupied at night, its mass walls are thinner than a residence's should be so that they will allow the heat to conduct to the occupied space by the evening (Figure 2.7).

Figure 2.7 Detail of a thermal storage wall. NREL's Visitors Center. Here, the thermal storage wall is a filled concrete block located about four inches behind the glass collector.

There is a variation of the thermal storage wall that is vented. In addition to using conduction, vented thermal storage walls also use convection (where air moves between the glass and mass wall and into living spaces). However, Ed Mazria states in *Solar Building Architecture* that vented thermal storage walls are no more effective than unvented ones. Plus, the space between glass and mass wall in vented thermal storage walls is difficult to keep clean and dry. Vented thermal storage walls also risk heat loss in the winter if their convective loop is not blocked from reversing every evening.

There are also more exotic kinds of indirect gain systems such as roof-ponds and transparent thermal insulation.

## SUNSPACE SYSTEMS

The last type of passive solar system this book will cover is the sunspace. Sunspace systems are the most common kind of isolated gain system and are very effective. Sunspaces work like an attached solar furnace. They work well in historic house retrofits, when one does not want tosignificantly alter most the walls of the existing house.

In sunspaces, the sunlight goes through the glass collector and hits the absorbers (walls and floor), which heats the air. This hot air rises (convection) and circulates into the living space, then falls as it cools and moves back into the sunspace to be heated again (Figure 2.8). This is a convective loop. Sunspace heat can also be mechanically ducted into living spaces.

During the summer, when cooling is important, convection allows heat to rise to the exterior out of high openings in the sunspace, creating a vacuum that pulls cool air through the living space.

SUNSPACE

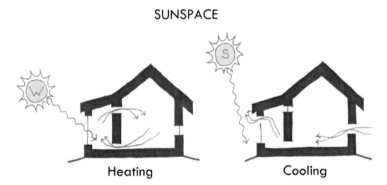

Heating                          Cooling

Figure 2.8 Sunspace System. In the winter (Heating) the sunlight goes through the sunspace's collector (glass) and hits an absorber (floor and walls), which heats the air. This hot air rises with convection into the living spaces. As air cools in the living space, it falls back into the sunspace. During the summer (Cooling), hot air is directed outside the building, pulling cool air through.

The wall between the sunspace and living areas needs to be insulated and its openings need to be closable to stop heat transfer when the sunspace is at an unhelpful temperature. Sunspaces should not be mechanically heated or cooled; their temperature should be allowed to fluctuate.

Sunspaces need high and low openings to allow convection to the living areas. The minimum area for openings is five square feet per 100 square feet of south glass, with opening areas divided as far apart as possible between high and low. To stop winter nighttime heat loss, these openings must be closed every evening with insulated covers. This natural convention can be enhanced with mechanical ventilation that ducts the winter heat to the living spaces. To exhaust summer heat, there also need to be high openings to the exterior of the sunspace.

Sunspaces are very efficient, but cannot always be occupied since they are usually too hot in the summer. Also, with all their glass, sunspaces will lose a lot of winter heat during the night. They can also obstruct southern views and light.

If you want to mitigate temperature swings in a sunspace so it can be occupied more often, use thermal mass in it (see chapter three). If you just want to use the sunspace as a heater for the house, you can just have thermal mass in the house.

Figure 2.9 The Bien+Jackson House in Denver, Colorado used a sunspace system on the back so that the historic structure would not be modified significantly.

An example of a sunspace can be found in the Bien+Jackson House in Denver, Colorado designed by Doerr Architecture (Figures 2.9, 2.10, 2.11). The Bien+Jackson House was a beautifully restored 1908 Victorian energy hog due to poor insulation and air leakage. We did not want to modify the historic architectural character of the home by modifying all its walls to add insulation and by punching new holes in them for solar collectors. Instead, we added a sunspace on the back so we could capture the free solar energy without destroying the historic character. This energy is then pumped into the old house. The Bien+Jackson House also uses direct gain passive solar in its new living spaces above the sunspace (Figure 3.5).

Figure 2.10 Example of a sunspace added to the back side of the historic Bien+Jackson House.

Figure 2.11 Interior of the sunspace of the Bien+Jackson House. High windows to exhaust summer heat. Brick and concrete are its thermal mass.

It is important to note that, although plants can be placed in sunspaces, sunspaces are not greenhouses. Plants like light from above (glass ceilings). As will be described in detail in the next chapters, a glass ceiling would make a sunspace too hot in the summer and too cold in the winter. In addition, plants will use and block energy that you need for the house.

There is also a much more complex kind of indirect gain system called a thermosiphon, or convective loop system.

Those are the three types of passive solar systems. In the next chapter, this book will describe building strategies that are central to all three systems.

# CHAPTER III

# PASSIVE SOLAR STRATEGIES

The following seven passive solar strategies are important to understand for each of the passive solar systems.

## STRATEGY ONE: BUILDING ORIENTATION

The first and most important passive solar strategy is building orientation. At latitude 40° north (northern Colorado), the sun only gets to 27° above the horizon on the winter solstice (Figure 3.1). The sun does not rise due east or set due west. It actually rises 30° south of east, and sets 30° south of west.

The time to collect the sun's energy in the heart of winter is very short and as much of it as possible must be used to heat the house. To do this, make sure nothing such as buildings, trees, or hills are blocking the sun when it gets above 15° on the horizon. This 15° is about the same as being ten feet higher than the solar collectors within 35 feet of them. In other words, the south glass of the building must receive sunlight between 9am and 3pm during the winter.

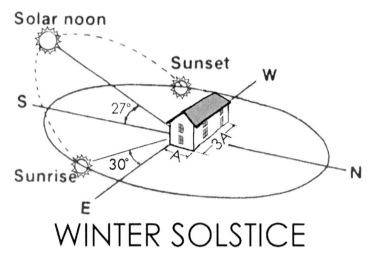

Figure 3.1 Sun path at the winter solstice at latitude 40° north. In the winter, the sun is mainly in the south, out for only a short time, and very low.

Even after deciduous trees drop their leaves, they can block over 60 percent of the sun's energy. This is why trees should not encroach into the sun's winter path, the south.

An excellent tool to determine the solar access of a certain location is the Solar Pathfinder (Figure 3.2). Solar Pathfinders can help determine where a building should be sited and where to place solar collectors and solar panels.

Figure 3.2 A Solar Pathfinder is a great tool to determine where and how significant obstructions to the sun are at a particular spot.

To capture the winter sun's energy and avoid the summer sun's, it is very important to locate the long dimension of a house facing within 20° of true south. This means a home should be longer along the east-west axis. If the long side of the house faces more than 20° off of true south, eight percent or more of the crucial winter sun's energy will be lost.

True south in Colorado is about ten degrees east of magnetic south, where the compass points (true north is about ten degrees west of magnetic north). Careful, magnetic south actually changes quite a bit year to year for the same location. Verify where true south is currently for your site at: ngdc.noaa.gov/geomag-web/#declination.

> **Tip:** Many green architects intentionally tilt houses ten degrees east of true south to jumpstart heating in the morning after a cold winter night.

A house with its long dimensions on the east and west has the worst orientation since it will get most of the sun's heat in the summer. Most of a home's glass should face south because not much winter sunlight comes from the north, east or west.

In the summer, the sun is high enough in the east and west to heat buildings—a problem (Figure 3.3). East and west windows have the worst orientations because, in the winter, they collect 1/3 as much solar radiation as the south collects. In the summer, east and west glass collect three times the radiation that the south collects. Plus when in the east and west, the sun comes in almost horizontally. Since it is difficult to block this horizontal light and in the winter little solar radiation goes to the east and west, it is best to minimize glass on these sides. Trees on the east and west sides can prevent some summer solar radiation from heating the building by blocking the horizontal rays.

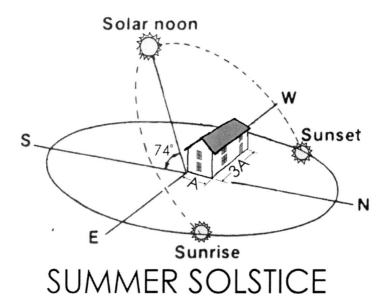

**Solar noon**

**W**

**S**

74°

**Sunset**

3A

A

**N**

**E**

**Sunrise**

# SUMMER SOLSTICE

Figure 3.3 Sun path at the summer solstice at latitude 40° north. The sun gets high above the horizon, rises north of east and sets north of west, potentially creating heating problems in the summer.

However, you can use the high path of the summer sun to control its heat on the south using the next strategy: solar shading.

## STRATEGY TWO: SOLAR SHADING

If you have oriented your house to maximize the collection of the southern sun's heat in the winter and minimize the sun's heat from the east and west, you then need to block southern sun's heat in the summer. This is quite simple with solar shading.

Figure 3.4    Traditional architectural elements such as these *vigas* (rough wood beams) with cross poles on the Moore NZE House can be used as sun shades.

With the sun very high to the south in the summer (Figure 3.3), solar shades easily block this solar radiation. Solar shades block the summer sun's rays externally so little heat enters the home. It is important to block heat externally because, once it gets in, it is a problem.

Figure 3.5 Solar shading can be simply done with roof overhangs as in the Bien+Jackson House. Notice the different depth of overhangs due to different roof angles and sill heights.

Solar shading must be designed to allow the low winter sunrays in to enter the southern glass and heat the building. Solar shades block the sun's rays starting in the spring, when heat becomes a problem, and through the summer. The solar shades begin to allow sunrays in again during the fall, when it becomes cold and the sun angle drops, allowing the sunrays to heat the space (Figure 3.6).

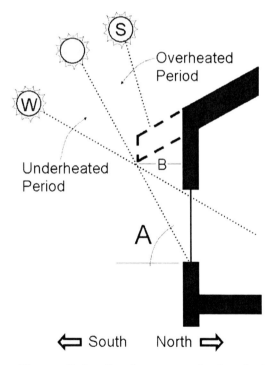

Figure 3.6    Southern sun shade design: Angle A (found in Table 3.1) determines how far out, B, the solar shade should project to the south so it blocks unwanted heat.

| Mean Winter Temperature | South Shade Angle A |
|---|---|
| 15°F (1500 HDD) | >74° |
| 20°F (1350 HDD) | 70° |
| 25°F (1200 HDD) | 66° |
| 30°F (1050 HDD) | 62° |
| 35°F (900 HDD) | 58° |
| 40°F (750 HDD) | 54° |
| Mean daily temperature (not mean highs or lows) in degrees Fahrenheit for December, January, and February. HDD = Heating degree days (base 65°) per average winter month, can be used instead of mean winter temperature. | |

Table 3.1 Southern solar shade design (angle A in Figure 3.6). Temperatures for many Colorado locations can be found in Appendix one. Others can be found online.

Examples of external solar shades include eaves, or roof overhangs (Figures 3.5, 3.10), trellises, awnings (Figure 1.2), external shutters, louvers, and arbors. These can be fixed or adjustable.

To block south facing glass from summer solar radiation, determine the depth, or projection, of the solar shade (B in Figure 3.6). For Colorado, Utah, Nevada, Nebraska, southern Wyoming, northern New Mexico, eastern Kansas, western Oklahoma, northeastern Arizona, and northwestern California, this depth is determined by angle A in Table 3.1.

To use Table 3.1, you will need to know the house site's mean, or average, winter temperature (mean of December, January, and February, not mean highs or lows). Mean winter temperatures for many Colorado locations are listed in Appendix one; others can be found online. Instead of mean winter temperature, HDD (heating degree days) base 65° for the winter months can be used. Angle A should start from the bottom of the glass that the shade is designed for.

For example: a house in Telluride, Colorado has a mean winter temperature of 21° (per Appendix one). In the left column of Table 3.1, find the closest mean winter temperature to 21°F (20°). To its right, the recommended southern shade angle A is 70°. Accordingly, you would build an eave, awning, or other solar shade that extends from the house to the line of 70° that starts at the sill of the window that the shade is designed for, see Figure 3.6.

Since 21° is higher than 20°, you could be more precise and make the solar shade angle 69°. However, you need not be exact with solar shading; just make sure you take advantage of the sparse winter sun and block the summer sun.

The angles in Table 3.1 are good to block most unwanted solar radiation. However, these angles also block some wanted solar gain in the spring.

This is due to the solar year and thermal year being out of sync, due to lag time caused by Earth's mass. An advanced technique is to improve the solar shades by making them moveable, or adjustable. To both block unwanted summer heat and allow all the desired spring sunlight, you would have to make the shade moveable so it allows 10°-15° more sunlight in the spring and even projects five degrees farther in the fall. Examples of moveable shades are awnings, rotating louvers and fins, external blinds, roller shades, and deciduous vegetation.

Since summer sunrays are fairly horizontal on the east and west, solar shades work very poorly on these exposures, unless the shades are operable, like adjustable louvers. Because of this, minimize east and west glass and do plant trees on these sides, not on the south.

You can test your solar shade designs by building them in a 3D modeling software with solar paths, such as SketchUp. SketchUp can show you how your solar shade will block the sun's rays at any given time.

## STRATEGY THREE: THERMAL MASS

Once you have allowed enough of the winter sun's heat in the home, how do you store this heat for the winter nights without overheating the house during the daytime? This was a common problem in early passive solar designs. The simple way to handle this is to use thermal mass.

Thermal mass is any dense material used inside a building to store heat. Thermal mass absorbs heat in the day so occupants do not overheat when the sun is out. Then, the mass slowly releases that stored heat all night. In this way, thermal mass reduces temperature swings.

Figure 3.7 Thermal mass can be beautiful such as this earthen floor, masonry, thick plaster, and tile on concrete.

During summer in areas with much cooler nights (big diurnal temperature swings), such as Colorado, thermal mass can keep a home cool by storing the night's coolness, or *coolth*, and releasing it during the day.

Examples of thermal mass—with the best listed first—are stone, brick, concrete, concrete block (filled), white oak, and adobe. Even multiple layers of gypsum board (drywall) help. Dark barrels filled with water are the best performing thermal mass, but they can leak and grow algae.

Thermal mass is most effective when spread throughout the house, not concentrated in one part. A depth of three to four inches of material is optimal. Greater than six inches of thickness will work against you. Thermal mass is most effective when it is located in walls and in the path of direct sunlight.

A good rule for the amount of thermal mass is three square feet or more of four-inch thick thermal mass for every square foot of southern glass. If little of your house's thermal mass is in the direct path of the sun, try to get at least six square feet of thermal mass per square foot of southern glass. More thermal mass area helps; more thermal mass depth does not help. If you cannot build the minimum amounts of mass described above, reduce the amount of southern glass recommended in the fourth strategy.

For example: if you have 380 square feet of glass on the south and the thermal mass will be partially in direct sunlight and a third of it will be in the walls (the norm), you can split the difference between the recommended three and six square feet of thermal mass and multiply the area of south glass by 4.5. Thus, you will need about 1710 (380 x 4.5) square feet of four-inch deep stone or brick.

Thermal mass is useless if it is covered with insulators. It is no problem using tile or plaster over thermal mass, but covering it with insulators, like carpet, negates its benefit.

**Tip:** Masonry fireplaces on the interior of a home can be great thermal mass. However, be sure to use a modern, efficient wood stove insert, since traditional fireplaces just send a home's heat up the chimney and pull in cold drafts.

If you do not invest in extra thermal mass, you cannot have a true passive solar home, but you can have a sun tempered home. A sun tempered home relies on the inherent thermal mass of typical construction and furnishings. Without the extra thermal mass, sun tempered homes cannot have as much south-facing glass as passive solar homes or they will overheat during the day and cool too much at night. Studies show that sun tempering can attain a 25 percent reduction in heating cost. To perform well, sun tempered houses should have southern glass equal to less than seven percent of the floor area, as described in the following section.

## STRATEGY FOUR: GLASS

The area of southern glass you use on a passive house depends on the area of its heated living, or conditioned, space (Figure 3.8) and the mean, or average, winter temperature (mean of December, January, and February, not mean highs or lows) of its site, multiplied by the percentage in Table 3.2. Instead of mean winter temperature, HDD (heating degree days) base 65° for the winter months can be used.

Figure 3.8  To determine the area of southern glass (grayed windows), multiply the floor area by the percentage in Table 3.2 (A x B x Floors x %)

| Mean Winter Temperature | South Glass Area per Floor Area |
|---|---|
| 15°F (1500 HDD) | 33%* |
| 20°F (1350 HDD) | 29%* |
| 25°F (1200 HDD) | 25% |
| 30°F (1050 HDD) | 21% |
| 35°F (900 HDD) | 17% |
| 40°F (750 HDD) | 13% |

Mean daily temperature (not mean highs or lows) in degrees Fahrenheit for December, January, and February.

HDD = Heating degree days (base 65°) per average winter month, can be used instead of mean winter temperature.

* With insulation over glass at night or U<0.1

Adapted from *The Passive Solar Energy Book* by Ed Mazria

Table 3.2 Southern glass (solar collector) area per heated living space per climate. Temperatures for many Colorado locations can be found in Appendix one. Others can be found online.

This southern glass area can be divided between direct gain, thermal storage wall, and sunspace systems. Sunspaces can use more southern glass since they are thermally isolated from living spaces and can direct any of their unwanted heat to the exterior.

For example, Steamboat Springs, Colorado has a mean winter temperature of 16°F. In table 3.2, in the left column, find the closest mean winter temperature to 16°F (15°). To its right, the recommended southern glass per conditioned floor area is 33 percent. For a 2000 square foot home, 660 (2000 x 0.33) square feet of south-facing glass will be required. Another way to look at this is that for every 1000 square feet of living space, a Steamboat house requires 320 square feet of solar collector. Since 16° is greater than 15°, you could be more precise and make the southern glass area 32 percent. Keep in mind, what is more important than the area of southern glass is balancing this area with thermal mass, as described in the third strategy.

Also note the asterisk in the table next to the percentages 29 and 33. This indicates that, since it is in a very cold climate and you want to avoid unacceptable nighttime heat loss, you need to use insulated window coverings, high-performance windows, or less glass.

For any glass area above 13 percent, solar pioneer Doug Balcomb recommends in *Passive Solar Buildings* that heat be gained through other passive solar systems, such as a thermal storage wall, to avoid sun-drenching, or glare.

**Energy Modeling Software**
Passive solar design decisions can be tested in energy modeling software such as Energy-10. However, personal experience and studies by Evan Mills of the Lawrence Berkeley National Lab and others show these programs to be quite inaccurate. This software is also complicated to use, so you will probably need to hire a specialist. In a few more years, energy modeling software will probably be helpful.

To provide adequate insulation for your home, all windows and glass doors should have at least two layers of glass, or glazing, and have a U-factor (thermal transmission value) of 0.35 or less for the entire window performance, including frame and spacer material (not just glass performance). U-factor is the reciprocal of R-value (thermal resistance value; $1/U=R$). For example, a U-0.35 would only equal about R-3. This is seven times worse at insulating than a normal wall. High-performance windows can get better than U-0.14 (R-7), but the high cost of these windows is hard to recoup.

**Tip:** Since windows are usually the worst insulating surfaces of a house, set aside money in your construction budget for insulated window coverings, such as cellular shades. Learn more about this in chapter four.

Low-e (low-emissivity) film with glass is a far better insulator than plain glass and low-e will also block damaging UV rays. Because of this, low-e film should be used in all windows. In cold climates such as Colorado, the low-e film, or coating, should be on the glass surface between the panes that is closest to the interior of the house. According to building scientist Paul Fisette, using low-e is almost as effective as adding another pane of glass. You can have the best of both worlds by selecting low-e on a separate film between the glass panes to create another insulating air space.

*Tune* glass to the solar orientation: choose a heat-reflective (not light-reflective) glass for the east and west sides since solar radiation on these sides is difficult to control. Heat reflection is measured as SHGC (Solar Heat Gain Coefficient). Eastern and western windows should have an SHGC of 0.25 or less. A 0.25 SHGC means that 75 percent of the heat will be reflected. Southern windows should have an SHGC of 0.6 or greater to allow solar radiation in since we control this radiation with solar shades.

**Tip:** When choosing differently *tuned* windows that will be near each other in the house, compare them in sunlight to see if their glass tints look different enough to be visually troubling.

To further improve a window's performance, glass panes can be filled with gasses such as argon and krypton. As a rule, hinged windows, such as casement and awning windows, air-seal better than slider windows. Fixed-glass windows air seal the best. You should specify windows with air leakage less than 0.30 US/I-P.

World's Best
Window Co.

National Fenestration
Rating Council®
CERTIFIED

Millennium 2000⁺
Vinyl-Clad Wood Frame
Double Glazing • Argon Fill • Low E
Product Type: **Vertical Slider**

**ENERGY PERFORMANCE RATINGS**

| U-Factor (U.S./I-P) | Solar Heat Gain Coefficient |
|---|---|
| **0.30** | **0.30** |

**ADDITIONAL PERFORMANCE RATINGS**

| Visible Transmittance | Air Leakage (U.S./I-P) |
|---|---|
| **0.51** | **0.2** |

Manufacturer stipulates that these ratings conform to applicable NFRC procedures for determining whole product performance. NFRC ratings are determined for a fixed set of environmental conditions and a specific product size. NFRC does not recommend any product and does not warrant the suitability of any product for any specific use. Consult manufacturer's literature for other product performance information.
www.nfrc.org

Figure 3.9   An NFRC label like this one tells what you need to know about a window's performance.

Good window manufacturers provide NFRC labels (Figure 3.9) rating their windows' SHGC, U-factor, air leakage, and other important information. You can compare window performance of different manufacturers at nfrc.org.

Figure 3.10 Instead of problem causing skylights, clearstory windows, like those shown on the Finch House above, can control what sunlight they let in with sun shades.

Skylights (horizontal and sloped glass) are a bad idea because they allow in the high summer sun's heat and glare. Skylights allow in four times more solar radiation in the summer than vertical glass does, and 1/3 of the radiation in the winter. This is the opposite of what you want. Also, skylights are very difficult to shade, screen, and insulate. Plus, skylights let out winter heat on a building's most important insulating surface, the roof, and they often have problems with dirt and leaks.

Pipes for sunlight, called sun tubes and many other names, are better than skylights because they are better insulators. Vertical glass, such as in clearstory windows (Figures 3.10, 3.14, 5.8) and dormers, is better than sloped glass or light tubes since you can control sunlight with solar shades and avoid the many problems.

## STRATEGY FIVE: VENTILATION

What about summertime cooling and getting fresh air in your passive solar home? When the temperature drops below 65° at night, a house can be cooled by opening high and low windows to create convection (hot air rising) to bring in the cool night air (Figure 3.11). This night air cools the thermal mass that will then absorb the summer heat all day. Just close the windows during the day and feel the *coolth*.

**Figure 3.11** Opening high and low windows at night in the summer allows hot air rising with convection to cool your house naturally.

If passive convection cannot be achieved in your design, you can cheat and install a well-insulated whole house fan that will exhaust the summer day's hot air.

Another passive cooling strategy is cross ventilation. Cross ventilation is created with windows on multiple sides of a room. This exhausts heat and creates air movement, which helps you to feel cooler even when the temperature is the same. To enhance ventilation, if there is a predominant summer wind direction, make the windows on the downwind side of the home larger.

Ceiling fans help the same way as cross ventilation does. In the summer, they create air movement to make us feel cooler. Ceiling fans can also help in the winter, if they are turned on low, by moving heat from the ceiling down to the floor level.

> **Tip:** If there is an attached garage, air seal it from the home and install a timed exhaust fan set to run for 10-15 minutes after the garage door closes. This will to get rid of your cars' toxic gasses.

If we build an air-tight home, how can we exhaust stale air without wasting its energy? HRVs (Heat Recovery Ventilators) and ERVs (Energy Recovery Ventilators) exhaust old air from tightly constructed homes without wasting much winter heat by using a very efficient air-to-air heat exchanger. In the winter, this heat exchanger preheats the incoming fresh air with the exhaust air, saving over 80 percent of the energy. ERVs (Figure 3.12) also control moisture in the air. HRVs and ERVs are a fairly inexpensive technology and a great way to save energy. So build tight and ventilate right.

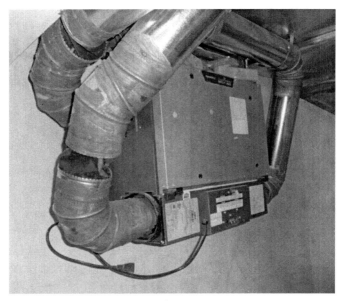

Figure 3.12 An ERV (Energy Recovery Ventilator) exhausts old air and brings in fresh air without wasting energy.

With multilevel homes and high ceilings, how can you stop the winter heat from staying in the high areas? A simple air destratification system uses a small fan motor and a duct to bring heat from up high in the house to down low. This is a great way to heat a basement with very little energy.

> **Tip:** Radon is a naturally occurring gas in the earth that is carcinogenic. According to The Florida Department of Health: "Radon is the primary cause of lung cancer among non-smokers and is the second leading cause of lung cancer after smoking." Consider roughing in plumbing for radon mitigation and, after the house is built, test for radon.

## STRATEGY SIX: ROOM ARRANGEMENT

A simple strategy to increase home comfort is good room arrangement. Locate frequently used spaces such as living and dining rooms on the south side. Locate infrequently used rooms, such as closets, pantries, garages, stairs, laundry, and utility rooms, on the north side and these will act as a buffer from the cold north winds. To avoid glare in rooms primarily used for viewing TV or computer monitors, you can place them on the north or in a basement.

Open floor plans allow heat to equalize throughout the house. Open floor plans also improve comfort by allowing balanced daylighting and cross-ventilation.

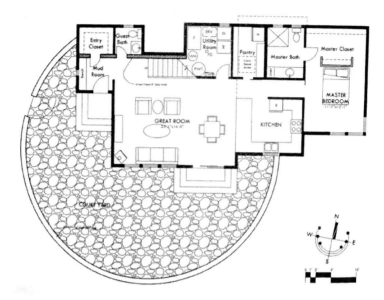

Figure 3.13 Rooms in the Finstad+Cash House were arranged by Doerr Architecture so that those frequently used are on the south. Infrequently used rooms act as a buffer to the north. The open floor plan makes the house feel larger and increases thermal comfort.

## STRATEGY SEVEN: DAYLIGHTING

The last passive solar strategy is the use of natural light from the sun, daylighting. Good daylighting can save over five percent of a typical home's energy usage by reducing the energy used by artificial lighting and the heat this creates.

The full spectrum light of the sun promotes health, reduces absenteeism, and increases productivity. Research by the Heschong Mahone Group shows that students perform about 20 percent better in classrooms that have better daylighting.

The potential problem with daylighting is glare. Glare is caused by horizontal light. To avoid glare, it is best to bring light in from high up with clearstory windows, like cathedrals do (Figures 3.14, 5.8).

Glare can also be addressed by balancing light, having it come from multiple sides of room. Bouncing light up with light shelves and blinds to bring light higher and deeper into a space also help. Circulation areas (open hallways) near the southern glass can also be used to bounce light up (as well as be an excellent spot for thermal mass).

Not only are skylights a bad choice for thermal performance, they are a bad choice for daylighting because their light is difficult to control. It is difficult to have window coverings on skylights so the sun will blast everything below them. In addition, horizontal glass collects dirt and is begging to leak. If light needs to come from above and clearstory windows will not work, consider more energy efficient pipes for sunlight called sun tubes and many other names.

Figure 3.14 The Moore NZE House shows how bringing in daylight from high with clearstory windows and from multiple sides can create pleasant lighting.

# CHAPTER IV

# OTHER GREEN BUILDING STRATEGIES

The following strategies are not only crucial to passive solar homes, they are crucial to any energy-efficient building. Without these strategies, a passive solar home will perform poorly.

## INSULATION AND THERMAL BREAKS

Insulation is one of the most important components of passive solar homes. It would be difficult to use too much insulation. Remember that code-required insulation is just the minimum.

In cold climates such as Colorado, wall insulation should have a R-value (thermal resistance value) of R-20 or higher, roofs should be at least R-38, crawl spaces should be at least R-19, floors over unheated spaces should be at least R-38, and basements and slabs should be at least R-10; the more, the better. Green homes usually exceed these levels by at least 50 percent.

With closed-cell spray foam's great air and moisture sealing, superior insulating value (R-6.5 per inch), and even structural properties, it is the insulation of choice for green homes (Figure 4.1). Closed-cell foam does costs more but, unlike other types of insulation, does not have air gaps or allow moisture to penetrate and reduce its performance.

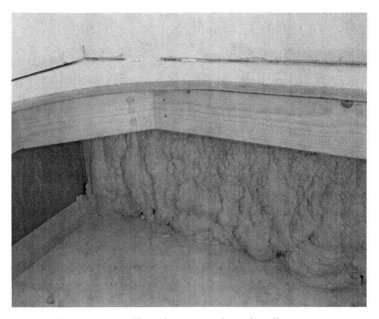

Figure 4.1 This shows a closed-cell spray foam insulation on an often overlooked area: between bathtubs and exterior walls. This type of insulation also acts as an air and moisture barrier.

**Tips:** To avoid a large energy loss, make sure any ductwork is within the insulated area of the house. If the ducts pass through any crawl space or attic, do not vent these spaces to the exterior. Seal the ducts from leakage with mastic.

Since windows are usually the poorest insulating component of a home by far, it is important to use insulating window coverings, such as cellular, or honeycomb, shades. Wood blinds, thermally lined draperies, and roman shades also help insulate. Fitting the covering into two tracks on the sides will increase its performance by a factor of four. Products such as quilted coverings and coverings that seal on all four sides provide another step up in efficiency, up to R-6. Coverings with light colored surfaces toward the window give the added benefit of reflecting summer heat gain.

When insulating, a common mistake is to forget about thermal bridging. Thermal bridging occurs when heat bypasses insulation by going through framing such as wood studs, see Figure 4.2. Wood is a poor insulator and wood makes up about 25 percent of a stud wall. Therefore, if the wood studs touch interior and exterior wall surfaces, heat can move through the studs despite insulation between the studs.

A thermal bridge can be broken by using walls with continuous insulation such as SIPs (structurally insulated panels), straw bale construction, and conventional stud framing covered with rigid insulation. An inexpensive way to stop thermal bridging and to have a thick cavity for insulation is to build parallel 2x4 stud walls with a gap between them. You then fill this entire cavity with insulation. These continuously insulated walls break the unwanted flow of heat.

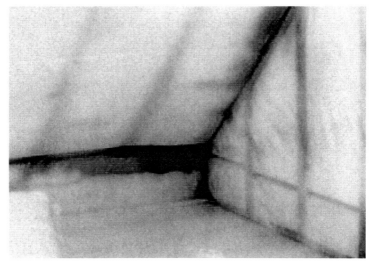

Figure 4.2 The dark areas in this infrared photo show where winter heat is being lost to thermal bridging through the studs.

When using roof trusses, make sure the most important insulation, the roof's, stays at full depth near the exterior walls. To have continuous insulation in the roof surfaces, use raised-heel trusses.

Contrary to old hippies' beliefs, dirt is a poor insulator. There are reasons to bury parts of buildings, but insulation is not one of them, nor are cost, ventilation, or daylighting.

## AIR SEALING

It does little good to insulate a building and then have air flow through gaps in the construction. This is called air infiltration. Air infiltration accounts for 20-30 percent of home energy loss, or about $450 per year. To avoid this waste, seal your home from air leaks. Specify sill gaskets, insulated can lights, outlet cover gaskets, and air-tight construction around windows and doors.

The quality of air sealing can easily be verified during construction with an inexpensive blower door test (Figure 4.3). If you have a blower door test done before the gypsum board is installed, you can locate leaks that then can be sealed. ACH (air changes per hour) is the amount of air inside your home that is replaced by outside air every hour. Ideally you want to get below 1.0 ACH at an air pressure of 50 pascals.

Figure 4.3    Get a blower door test to determine how well your home is air sealed.

There is a concern that tightly sealed homes will lack fresh air and have poor IAQ (Indoor Air Quality). IAQ should not be addressed by building leaky, energy inefficient homes. Instead, build tight and ventilate right. If you achieve 0.35 ACH or less, add controlled ventilation without wasting energy with an HRV (Heat Recovery Ventilator) or an ERV (Energy Recovery Ventilator) described in the previous chapter under ventilation.

**Clarification of terms:** a Passivhaus, or Passive House, is not necessarily a passive solar house, but it can be. The Passive House Institute promotes a type of super-insulated and air-sealed building that meets rigorous energy consumption criteria; they are about equivalent to a HERS 15 (85% less energy use than standard houses).

## LIGHT-COLORED ROOFS

Light-colored roofs reflect the unwanted high summer sun's heat. According to a Lawrence Berkeley National Laboratory physicist, dark colors on a 1000 square foot roof cause an extra ten metric tons of carbon dioxide emissions due to the extra cooling they necessitate. Dark roofs cause 15 percent more cooling costs in the summer. So, select white or light-colored shingles, roof tiles, roof membranes, and metal roofs.

## SOLAR HOT WATER

Of a typical home's energy bill, 25 percent is for hot water. Solar thermal is a cost-effective and green way of creating hot water. Solar thermal is an active solar system that uses the sun to heat water with panels or evacuated tubes (Figure 4.4) usually placed on roofs. Solar thermal usually pays for itself in a few years and then the rest of your water heating is free.

Figure 4.4   Solar thermal tubes for hot water are in the front and PV panels for electricity are in the back.

To accommodate solar thermal, design a south facing roof at an angle of at least 40°; the site's latitude plus 10° is ideal. Allow room for at least two 4'x8' solar thermal panels. If you plan to use the solar hot water for more than normal uses (showers, laundry, and dishes) make room for more panels. Extra uses include radiant floors, water-to-air heat exchangers, and hot tubs. There will be more hot water storage required, usually a second tank, so allow space for this. Using the solar heated water for space heating requires large insulated tanks; the

Moore NZE House uses a 1200 gallon reclaimed stainless steel milk tank. A solar thermal installer can size the system for your needs.

## SOLAR ELECTRIC

The largest portion of human carbon dioxide emission is due to electrical use because most electricity comes from coal burning power plants. Any strategy to create electricity that avoids burning coal or creating nuclear waste is better. Solar electric, or PV (photovoltaic), is an active solar system of cells, which are usually in panels, and equipment that converts sunlight into electricity.

PV panels should face south but have a wide tolerance for their angle from horizontal and can even be located off the building (Figure 4.4). A normal American home's electrical use is about two watts per square foot. Thus, a four kiloWatt system is enough for most 2000 square foot homes. However, the system should be designed by a solar installer for the specific house. Energy conscious occupants can get by with less than half of the norm.

You can have a grid-tied solar electric system that uses the electrical grid as storage. With a grid-tied system, you feed the grid during the day and take back power at night. With net metering, your electric meter will spin backward when your PV system is producing more electricity than you are using.

Your PV system can also be off the electrical grid with battery storage. Off-grid systems are more expensive than grid-tied systems, but they are usually less expensive than paying the utility company to extend power lines over a quarter mile to a home site. Your bank of batteries will need a temperature-controlled (70°F) and vented room. Batteries also require regular maintenance and will need to be replaced every five to ten years.

There are also more expensive PV systems that combine grid-tied and battery storage as backup for when the electric grid goes down.

**Tip:** Other types of renewable energy are trickier than PV. Using wind turbines to generate electricity only works in a small percentage of locations and, even then, is extremely site specific; you will need to test your site. Fuel cells have started being used in buildings but are not widely available at the moment. If you have a stream on your site, micro hydro power may be an option. You can learn more about renewable energy systems in Johnston and Gibson's book, *Toward a Zero Energy Home*.

Solar electric is quite expensive, but there are often federal and local incentives to lower the cost. Most homes are financed and often the monthly cost of a photovoltaic system can be mostly offset by electricity savings. Plus, all your electricity will then be free and not creating carbon dioxide.

## BUILDING SIZE

Invest your money in beautiful, well-designed, green homes, not in gigantic, resource-intensive ones that you will have to pay oodles to build, heat, cool, furnish, and clean. Build high-quality, not high-quantity, as Sarah Susanka describes in her book, *The Not So Big House*.

## HOME LOCATION

Generate fewer and shorter car trips to reduce pollution by locating homes near other places the occupants need to get to regularly, such as work, grocery stores, cafes, and schools. This has the added benefits of giving the occupants more free time and savings from less driving. Plus, they may get healthier from walking and biking more.

## EFFICIENT APPLIANCES AND LIGHTING

Minimize the amount of energy you need. Using high-efficiency appliances and lighting is a good way to reduce energy use and save money. Examples include high-efficiency boilers and furnaces with up to 97 percent AFUE (annual fuel utilization efficiency), low-flow water fixtures, compact fluorescent and LED lighting, and, most importantly, high-efficiency refrigerators. To ensure you are getting better performing appliances, only purchase ones labeled by the US Department of Energy as "Energy Star"(Figure 4.5).

Figure 4.5 The Energy Star label designates energy efficient appliances.

If your location requires more cooling than passive solar can handle, use an evaporative cooler. Evaporative coolers, also called swamp coolers, can save three to four times the energy used by conventional air conditioners.

For the small percentage of the time when passive solar is insufficient to keep your house comfortable, you will need to have a secondary heating system. Since this secondary heating system will get such little use, an inexpensive system such as a forced air furnace is a good choice. Why use a Mercedes to drive around the block when a VW will do? Forced air furnaces have a fast response time and have the added benefit of having ductwork that can do double duty as a fresh air delivery system.

> **Tip:** Choose a sealed, or closed, combustion furnace and a direct-vented hot water heater to avoid potential for carbon monoxide poisoning.

You can make forced air furnaces much more efficient by heating their air with solar heated water and a water-to-air heat exchanger, as was done in the Moore NZE House.

Another energy-efficient backup heating system is radiant floors, which are simply tubes of warm water circulating in the floor. Radiant floor systems are quite comfortable since their radiant heat comes from below and you do not have cold floors. They are also very energy-efficient. However, radiant floors are expensive to install and are not ideal to pair with passive solar due to their using the thermal mass of the floor that passive solar needs. More importantly, they have a very slow response time. It can take days for the radiant floor to get warm when all you usually need with your passive solar home is a burst of heat in the morning. An added cost due to a radiant floor system will be a separate ducting system for fresh air.

Radiant floor systems can be made even more efficient by heating the water they use with solar thermal panels or geothermal heating systems called ground source heat pumps. Ground source heat pumps can also cool a building economically. When a site does not have good solar access, this is a great system.

Modern wood stoves and masonry heaters, also called Russian stoves, are great, low-polluting, supplemental heat sources. However, they do not work automatically with a thermostat, so building departments will not count them as sufficient. Traditional fireplaces just send heat up the chimney, which pulls cold drafts into the house. If you want the look of a traditional fireplace, install an efficient wood or gas stove fireplace insert. To improve performance further, get the combustion air directly from the exterior.

## LOCAL AND GREEN MATERIALS

The last strategy: use locally produced green materials and products. Local production means that little fuel is used to bring in materials. However, you must weigh this against the environmental and performance benefits of materials and products brought in from a distance.

We spend over 90 percent of our lives indoors. Indoor air quality, IAQ, is usually many, many times worse than outdoor air quality. This is why it is important to use green materials that will not off-gas toxins that you then have to breath. Use low VOC (volatile organic compound) paints, finishes, construction adhesives, carpets, and pads. Do not use Liquid Nails. Choose cabinets made without urea formaldehyde.

In the next chapter, you will see how these strategies were used together in a case study of a passive solar house.

# CHAPTER V

# CASE STUDY

To help you understand how passive solar systems and strategies can be applied, we will look at a case study of a passive solar home, the Finch House. The Finch House is an addition and remodel in Denver, Colorado designed by Doerr Architecture and constructed by Ecofutures Building.

Holle Finch, had an existing international-style house that was very energy inefficient and had a leaking roof (Figure 5.1). An infrared thermometer showed that the windows were actually better insulators than the walls, since the windows had been updated and the walls were just double layers of masonry with no insulation.

In addition to addressing these issues, Holle wanted to add a bedroom and remodel the old kitchen and bathroom.

The passive solar system chosen for the Finch House was a direct gain system due to this system's low cost and the small area this system required on the tiny lot. A sunspace or even a thermal storage wall would have been difficult to squeeze onto this small site. This direct gain system's thermal collectors are its windows and its absorbers and thermal mass are its floors and walls—simple and cost effective.

Figure 5.1    Before: prior to being remodeled, the house, pictured here, was an energy hog with a leaking roof.

The original house had proper building orientation: the long side of house faced true south and its short sides faced east and west. The second-floor addition enhanced the proper orientation. We added a lot of glass on the south for winter heat gain and just a little on the east and west to avoid summer heat gain. Despite a neighboring building close to the south blocking winter sunlight, the required 15° of clear solar access was achieved by placing the solar collectors, clearstory windows, up high (Figures 5.2 & 5.3).

Figure 5.2 Proper solar access was attained, despite the adjacent building close to the south, by adding clearstory windows as high solar collectors where they would not be blocked.

The area of glass on the south needed for a passive solar house with proper thermal mass in Denver's climate, with a mean winter temperature of 31°F (Appendix one), is 21 percent of its floor area (per Table 3.2). For the 1607 square feet of living space, 338 (1607 x 0.21) square feet of south glass was ideal. Due to the layout of the existing house, we did not get quite this much.

One of the most noteworthy aspects of the Finch House's passive solar design is its use of clearstory windows to bring winter heat to the middle of the house (Figures 5.3, 5.8). This heat can then more easily flow to rooms on the north side of the house, so that not only the south side is warmed. Having thermal mass in walls avoids the common problem of the thermal mass in floors being covered with insulators such as carpet and furniture.

For solar shading in Denver, the southern roof overhangs were sized to block the sun when it gets over 62° above the horizon (per Table 3.1). With this angle, when it starts to get hot in the spring, the eaves block sunrays from entering through the glass. When it starts to get cold in fall (September), the eaves allow the low sunrays in to heat the house. The main sill heights determined where this angle started (Figure 5.3). Note the different eave depths due to the eaves having differing angles and being at different heights from the sills.

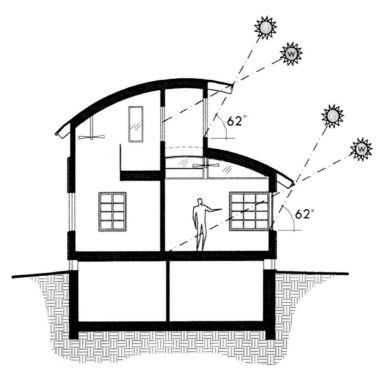

Figure 5.3 A direct gain passive solar system was built with overhangs designed to block the sunrays in the overheated period and to allow winter sunrays (W) all the way into the center of the house.

The design of the house was inspired by the lines in Holle's ceramics. With its dynamic vaults, the design also expresses an unfolding, or emergence. A welcoming porch was added to the front to contribute to the humaneness of the neighborhood. The garage was placed back on the alley, de-emphasizing cars.

Masonry is a poor insulator, but is great thermal mass. By encasing the old masonry walls in insulation, the masonry was effectively moved to the interior of the wall so it could be used as excellent thermal mass. This thermal mass is spread throughout the house, much in the direct path of the sun and most in the walls. "Moving" the thermal mass was achieved by encasing the masonry in with an impressive R-7 per inch rigid insulation called Polyisocyanurate. The Finch House's above ground thermal mass is six inches thick and seven times the area of its southern glass—more than enough (see chapter three).

Figure 5.4 The trees in the east shade the few eastern windows well and there are just a few north windows.

To better insulate, the windows are double pane glass, low-e with a U-factor of 0.30. To allow in winter heat and reject summer heat, the glass is *tuned* with a low SHGC (0.25 Solar Heat Gain Coefficient) on the east and west and a high SHGC (0.6) on the south.

Summer ventilation is achieved by using high windows, which allow natural convection to take heat up to escape all night and to pull cool night air across the thermal mass (Figure 5.5). Then, the thermal mass cools the house all day.

Figure 5.5    Operable high and low windows allow summer heat to rise and escape, pulling in cool air.

Ceiling fans help move air for summer cooling and bring warm air down for winter heating. To bring warm air from the upper floor down into the basement in the winter, an air destratification system was designed. This destratification system was simply a chase with a duct and an efficient Panasonic fan motor to pull warm air down to the basement.

Figure 5.6 On the west side, there is little glass and it is *tuned* with a low SHGC glass to reflect summer heat gain.

To take advantage of the sun in the winter, the room arrangement of the Finch House places the most frequently used rooms, such as dining and living rooms, on the south (Figure 5.7). Infrequently used rooms, such as the bathroom and utility room, are on the north. To avoid glare on computer monitors, the study was also placed on the north. The floor plan is open to make it more thermally comfortable and to help with air movement.

The Finch house uses natural daylighting to provide healthy sunlight and save the energy of artificial light. To alleviate glare, sunlight is brought in high with clearstory windows as old cathedrals do (Figures 5.8, 5.9). This clearstory light washes down the wall to the living space. In addition, most rooms have glass on two sides for balanced light.

In addition to the rigid insulation encasing the old masonry, new wall cavities were filled with a spray foam insulation, which also acts as an air barrier (Figure 5.10).

This is a high-quality, but not high-quantity, house of only 1607 square feet. By designing a *not-so-big house*, there is less material used and less house to pay to build, furnish, heat, and clean.

The Finch House is located near jobs, shopping areas, and schools to eliminate the need for many car trips. These adjacencies save money and reduce pollution. Locating her home near places she needs to get to regularly gives Holle more free time and opportunities to get exercise by walking and riding her bike on errands.

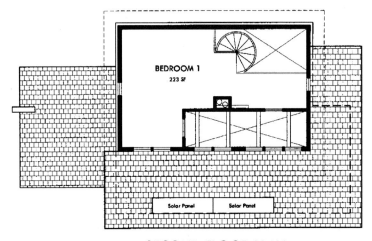

**SECOND FLOOR PLAN**

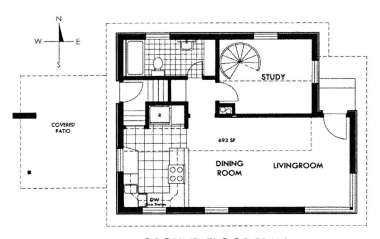

**GROUND FLOOR PLAN**

Figure 5.7 These floor plans show that the most frequently used rooms are on the south and an open floor plan to maximize thermal comfort and to help make the house feel bigger.

Figure 5.8 Glare-free daylighting is created with clearstory windows and windows on multiple sides. Photo by Holle Finch.

Figure 5.9 Clearstory windows bring the winter sun's energy deep into the house. Photo by Holle Finch.

Figure 5.10 The white material is a spray foam insulation, which also seals air leaks and adds structural support.

Existing materials, such as the masonry walls, were salvaged rather than being sent to a landfill, where all their embodied energy would have been wasted.

A good portion of the roof is oriented to the south at a good angle for solar thermal and PV panels to work very effectively.

To save energy, efficient appliances such as a two drawer dishwasher and compact fluorescent fixtures were selected. A low-flow toilet was installed to save water. For secondary heating, the house uses a forced air furnace that is 93.5 percent efficient and sealed combustion (no carbon monoxide risk). This forced air furnace also delivers fresh air.

To protect indoor air quality, renewable cork flooring and low off-gassing materials, such as Neil Kelly cabinets (no urea formaldehyde) and low VOC paint, construction adhesives, and finishes, were used.

You can see that, even with the difficulties of remodeling an existing house and having limited solar access, it is possible to create a beautiful home that treads quite lightly on the earth. Imagine how much easier it would be to do this with a new home. Even the new ceramics studio off the alley in back is passive solar.

Holle now has a home that fits her space needs and her aesthetics, and saves her energy costs while assuring she is comfortable despite any energy instability. Plus, as requested, her home now has a roof that does not leak. However, now she has to deal with the paparazzi; as she says, "We can hardly stand in our yard without a passersby commenting on the beautiful and unusual design."

With its award-winning aesthetics, wonderful daylighting, and green design, the Finch House is proof that you do not have to sacrifice beauty or comfort to live sustainably.

Figure 5.11 The award-winning passive solar Finch House designed by Doerr Architecture.

# CHAPTER VI

# SUMMARY

Passive solar design is a very effective and simple way to save money and minimize our biggest impact on the environment—buildings. To save most of the energy a building uses, apply passive solar design to heat it, as well as to cool, light, and ventilate it. By not requiring energy from fossil fuels and nuclear reactors, passive solar homes will save money, ensure your family's comfort, and be less of a burden on the planet.

There are three key types of passive solar systems: direct gain, thermal storage walls, and sunspaces. Each of these systems has its own advantages. With direct gain systems, the house's windows act as solar collectors and the walls and floors act as solar absorbers; this is why direct gain is the simplest and least expensive passive solar system. Thermal storage wall systems are good for rooms where you do not want as much light or where you want more privacy. Sunspace systems are great for additions to historic homes because you do not have to modify the home too much. These three systems can, and often should, be used on the same house.

The most important passive solar design strategy is to get proper building orientation, especially making sure your site has good southern solar access and laying out the house so that its long side faces south. Another important strategy is to design solar shades so that they allow in the winter's solar radiation and block the summer's. The other essential strategies are getting proper thermal mass, glazing, ventilation, room arrangement, and daylighting.

Insulation and air sealing are critical in any building. Use light-colored roofs, do not build more than you need, locate the home near where the occupants need to go, chose efficient appliances and lighting, and select local and green materials. Solar hot water and solar electric are great, but only for achieving what you cannot with less expensive passive solar design.

If you want to save money, your health, and the planet—if you want a truly green home—use these simple passive solar systems and strategies in the design of your house. Given how simple and effective passive solar is to use in the western states, it would be silly not to.

# MEAN WINTER TEMPERATURES FOR COLORADO

The following are mean, or average, daily temperatures (not mean highs or lows) in degrees Fahrenheit for December, January, and February for Colorado locations. These or mean winter HDD (heating degree days) will help you determine the proper solar shading angle and area of southern glass. The data is from NOAA (National Oceanic and Atmospheric Administration) "Climatology of the US No. 81" 1971-2000.

Verify online that the temperatures below are still current. If your house's location is not listed below, search ncdc.noaa.gov and other climate websites, then compare what you find to the nearest location below and the following map, Figure A1.1.

| | |
|---|---|
| AKRON 28° | ALTENBERN 26° |
| ALAMOSA 18° | ANTERO RES. 16° |

ASPEN 23°

BAILEY 24°

BERTHOUD PASS 13°

BLANCA 21°

BOULDER 34°

BRIGGSDALE 28°

BRIGHTON 32°

BROWNS PARK REF. 24°

BUENA VISTA 26°

BURLINGTON 30°

BYERS 28°

CAMPO 34°

CANON CITY 36°

CASTLE ROCK 30°

CHEESMAN 25°

CHEYENNE WELLS 32°

CIMARRON 20°

CLIMAX 14°

COLLBRAN 25°

COLORADO SPRINGS 30°

CORTEZ 29°

CRAIG 20°

CRESTED BUTTE 11°

CRESTONE 25°

DEL NORTE 22°

DELTA 29°

DENVER 31°

DILLON 17°

DURANGO 28°

EAGLE 23°

ESTES PARK 29°

EVERGREEN 28°

FLORISSANT FOSSIL 22°

FORT COLLINS 31°

FORT MORGAN 28°

FRUITA 28°

GLENWOOD SPRNGS 27°

GRAND JUNCTION 31°

GRAND LAKE 19°

GRANT 22°

GREELEY 30°

GUNNISON 13°

HAYDEN 21°

HERMIT 15°

HOLLY 31°

HOLYOKE 29°

IGNACIO 27°

JOES 29°

JULESBURG 30°

KARVAL 30°

| | |
|---|---|
| KAUFFMAN 27° | OURAY 25° |
| KIT CARSON 28° | PAGOSA SPRINGS 24° |
| KREMMLING 14° | PALISADE 32° |
| LA JUNTA 34° | PAONIA 30° |
| LAKE CITY 19° | PARKER 31° |
| LAKE GEORGE 17° | PUEBLO 31° |
| LAKEWOOD 30° | RANGELY 21° |
| LAMAR 31° | RED FEATHER LAKES 23° |
| LAS ANIMAS 33° | RIFLE 27° |
| LEADVILLE 18° | RYE 27° |
| LIMON 29° | SAGUACHE 21° |
| LINDON 28° | SALIDA 28° |
| LITTLE HILLS 21° | SAN LUIS 21° |
| LONGMONT 29° | SILVERTON 15° |
| LOVELAND 30° | SPRINGFIELD 32° |
| MANASSA 22° | STEAMBOAT SPRGS 16° |
| MAYBELL 19° | STERLING 28° |
| MONTE VISTA 20° | TACONY 32° |
| MONTROSE 28° | TAYLOR PARK 10° |
| MONUMENT 28° | TELLURIDE 21° |
| MT EVANS 16° | TRINIDAD 36° |
| NEDERLAND 25° | TWIN LAKES RES. 18° |
| NORTHDALE 25° | URAVAN 32° |
| NORTHGLENN 32° | VAIL 16° |
| NORWOOD 27° | WALDEN 19° |

WALSENBURG 36°

WALSH 33°

WESTCLIFFE 23°

WHEAT RIDGE 33°

WOLF CREEK PASS 18°

WRAY 30°

YAMPA 19°

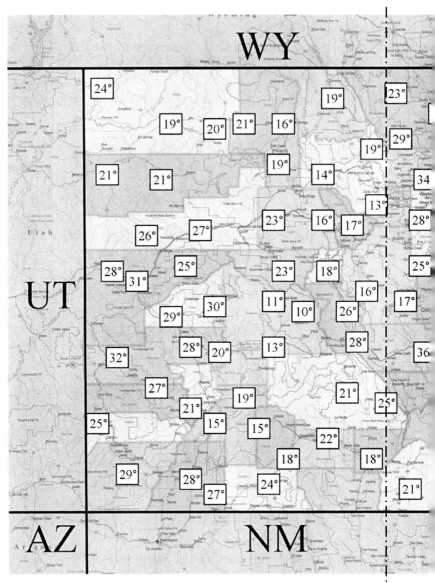

Figure A1.1 Map of mean winter temperatures in Colorado. Shown are mean (average) daily temperatures (not mean highs or lows) in degrees Fahrenheit for December, January, and February.

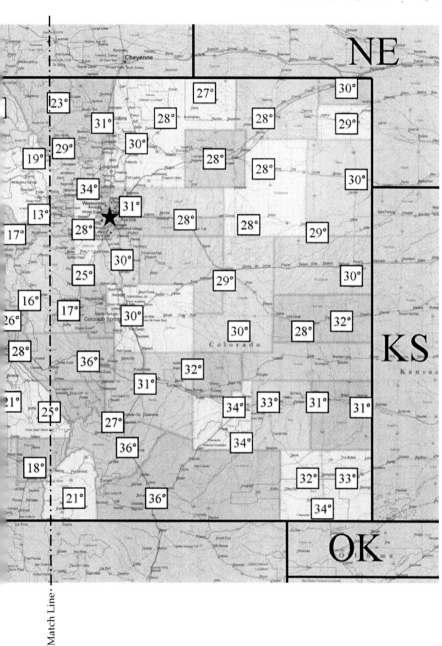

# WHERE TO GET MORE INFORMATION

## Builder's Guide: Cold Climates

by EEBA

A great technical manual on proper home construction for each climate type, a perfect companion to this book.

## Solar Home Tours

See what is being built near you. For tours, check the ASES (American Solar Energy Society) website, ases.org.

## Green Points or LEED Certified Architects

Design professionals that are not just talking the green talk; they have been tested. LEED stands for Leadership in Energy and Environmental Design.

## *Green Architecture Checklist: Residential*

by Colorado AIA-Committee on the Environment

A brief paper for you to check to make sure you covered the bases of green building. Available at doerr.org/services/residential-checklist.html

## NOAA

For detailed information on climatic information for US cities, surf ncdc.noaa.gov.

To determine true north, versus magnetic north, surf ngdc.noaa.gov/geomag-web/#declination

## Building America Best Practices Series

by US Department of Energy (DOE)

Lots of good free green building information at eere.energy.gov/topics/homes.html

## The Passive Solar Energy Book

by Edward Mazria

A good technical and comprehensive book on passive solar design.

## Toward a Zero Energy Home

by Johnston and Gibson

A good book about active solar and other renewable energy systems.

## BuildSustainably.com

Doerr Architecture's website has green building resources as well as Thomas Doerr's contact information for speaking, seminars, and consulting.

# INDEX

"Save the planet—it's our only source of chocolate!"

-Unknown

**Discuss and Get Copies of this Book**

You can find links to join the *Passive Solar Simplified* Facebook discussion and links to contact the author with any questions or comments at PassiveSolarSimplified.com. Also, copies of this book can be ordered from this website, as well as from Amazon.com and local bookstores.

CPSIA information can be obtained at www.ICGtesting.com
Printed in the USA
BVOW012209210213

313930BV00007B/63/P